Rookie
Read-About® Holidays

Chanukah

By David F. Marx

Consultant
Katharine A. Kane, Reading Specialist
Former Language Arts Coordinator
San Diego County Office of Education

Children's Press®
A Division of Grolier Publishing
New York   London   Hong Kong   Sydney
Danbury, Connecticut

Visit Children's Press® on the Internet at:
http://publishing.grolier.com

Designer: Herman Adler Design Group
Photo Researcher: Caroline Anderson

Library of Congress Cataloging-in-Publication Data

Marx, David F.
    Chanukah / by David F. Marx.
      p. cm. — (Rookie read-about holidays)
    Includes index.
    Summary: Introduces the history, customs, meaning, and celebration of
Chanukah.
    ISBN 0-516-22204-X (lib. bdg.)   0-516-27152-0 (pbk.)
    1. Hanukkah—Juvenile literature. [1. Hanukkah. 2. Holidays.] I. Title.
    BM695.H3M28   2000
    296.4'35—dc21   00-022633

Do you celebrate Chanukah?

3

Chanukah (HAHN-oo-kuh) lasts eight nights every winter. The exact dates change from year to year.

December 2000

Sunday	Monday	Tuesday	Wednesday	Thursday	Friday	Saturday
					1	2
3	4	5	6	7	8	9
10	11	12	13	14	15	16
17	18	19	20	21	22	23
24	25	26	27	28	29	30/31

Chanukah always comes sometime in December.

December 2001

Sunday	Monday	Tuesday	Wednesday	Thursday	Friday	Saturday
						1
2	3	4	5	6	7	8
9	10	11	12	13	14	15
16	17	18	19	20	21	22
23/30	24/31	25	26	27	28	29

Celebrating Chanukah in a faraway city

Chanukah is a holiday celebrated by people of the Jewish religion. Jewish people live in countries all over the world.

Chanukah is called the "Festival of Lights." On each night of this holiday, families light candles.

The candles are held in a menorah (muh-NOR-uh).

9

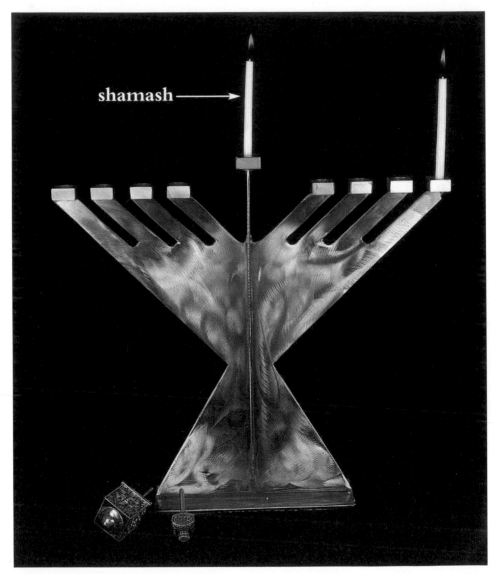

shamash ──────→

The candle in the middle is the shamash.

10

The menorah holds nine
candles. There is one
candle for each of the
eight nights, plus the
shamash (SHAH-mush).
"Shamash" means servant,
or helper.

An adult lights the shamash with a match. Then, a child lights all the other candles with the shamash.

13

On the first night
of Chanukah,
you light just
the shamash and
one other candle.

First Night

On the second
night, you light
the shamash and
two other candles.

Second Night

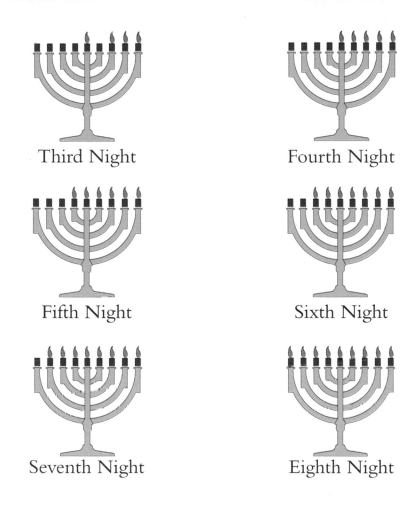

Third Night

Fourth Night

Fifth Night

Sixth Night

Seventh Night

Eighth Night

On the eighth night, all nine candles glow.

How did Chanukah start?
It began with a battle many
years ago.

Jewish people called
Maccabees (MACK-uh-beez)
were fighting another group
called Syrians (SEER-ee-uhns).

The Syrians tried to force
the Maccabees to stop
being Jewish.

The Maccabees fought bravely.

The Maccabees were
brave and strong.

They won their battle.

Today's Chanukah
celebrates their victory.

Jewish families and friends get together during Chanukah for parties.

They eat special foods, sing happy songs, give presents, and play games.

21

Potato pancakes fried in oil and served with applesauce are a favorite Chanukah food. They are called latkes (LAHT-kuhz).

Latkes and applesauce

23

Some kids like to play
dreidel (DRAY-del). In
this game, you take turns
spinning a top with four
sides called a dreidel.

Each side of the dreidel
shows a different Hebrew
letter. Hebrew is the
special language of
the Jewish people.

dreidel ———————→

People play dreidel with coins, beans, or pieces of candy. First, everyone throws one coin into the pot. Players then take turns spinning the dreidel.

gimel
take all of the coins

hay
take half of the coins

The letter that lands faceup tells them what to do next. When someone wins the whole pot, the game is over.

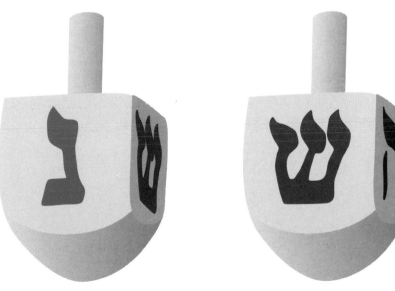

nun
take nothing

shin
put two coins in

Children love getting
presents on Chanukah.

The best present of all
is having fun with your
family and celebrating
for eight special nights.

29

Words You Know

dreidel

Hebrew

latkes

Maccabees

menorah

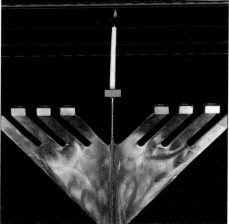

shamash

Index

About the Author

David F. Marx is an author and editor of children's books. He resides in the Chicago area.

Photo Credits

Photographs ©: Corbis-Bettmann: 29 (James L. Amos), 22 (Dennis Degnan); PhotoEdit: 3, 21 (Myrleen Ferguson), 10, 30 bottom (Jeff Greenberg), 13 (Michael Newman), 14, 30 top (A. Ramey); Superstock, Inc.: 9, 30 center (David David Gallery, Philadelphia); Tony Stone Images: 25, 31 bottom left (Peter Cade), 18 (Jim Corwin), 5 (Paul Damien), 17, 31 top right (Julie Marcotte), 6, 31 bottom right (Robert Van Der Hilst), cover (Craig Wells), 26, 31 top left (Trevor Wood).